The Art of Wisdom

Poems for Soul Growth

Françoise Hélène

Françoise Hélène

ILLUSTRATIONS BY AMY FORD & NINA JAYA
COVER DESIGN BY GANEERO.ART

www.francoisehelene.com

ISBN: 978-1-7399500-0-2

It took a lot of love and a lot of pain to write this book.

It is inspired by my life experiences (which have been transformed into metaphors), my feelings and my sense of empathy, which you will find a lot of in chapter two. It is also influenced and inspired by one of my grandmothers, who passed away when I was a child.

This book holds my hopes, my dreams, my desires, my values, my thoughts, passions, fears, struggles, my imagination, pieces of my reality and a lot of my soul, which is always intertwined with light and darkness.

I hope this book brings you reflection and leaves you lingering in deep thoughts. But, mostly, I hope it takes you on an engaging and emotional journey, and that you learn something from it and it touches a piece of your heart, somewhere along the way.

Here is a piece of mine.

With love & sorrow (mostly love)

Françoise Hélène

A work of art is created by a person's thoughts,
who develops and transforms them into the concrete.
Though a soul forever remains
the original piece of art itself.

Françoise Hélène

Table of Contents

Grandma's Story

I grew up in a small, quaint French village where we seldom saw people passing by our living room window in the morning. It was a quiet place where the sea was a highlight of Sunday aftenoons, a reflective place that brought peace to my heart.

We were rich with land, a space that remained the same in my eyes despite the changes in society, year after year. It was a place growing with modern time, and I allowed it to be what it was meant to be. Beyond my years, I never wondered what it would eventually become because it was perfect when I lived there, and I knew we'd both have disappeared into dust before it became something new, remembered for the beauty of our simplicity.

Growing up, I learnt to cherish the natural beauty of the world. Our backyard was covered with flowers of every kind and I would pick some in the summer to decorate our wooden dining table.

Canadian winters embraced the cold and we had our own ice rink ten steps from the house, and I'd spend evenings skating, listening to music and gazing at stars.

The Land

A land lived, once,
of lavish corn
and golden rivers,
among the grass -
sunrise-coloured:
chariots, horses
and warriors.

Once the home of bravery
and sacrifice,
nourishing the world
through natural splendour,
serving wheat as morning savour
and rich in elegance, eminent skies
and moonlights
providing shelters for wild animals,
farmers and knights.

Here, once danced happiness
and sorrow,
forgotten footsteps
lost in the Milky Way,
blissful on the horizon,
luminous in twilight,
lonely as the darkness of the shadow
of nights fading,
reborn as an ancient city,
now breathing through the ancestors
of a tree.

I lived a simple life where our main entertainments were books and magazines from my bedroom's library, local music events at the beach and walks in the forests. I loved spending time in nature, it inspired peace within me. The trees, rivers, mountains and birds were my everyday doctors. Besides my birthday, two very exciting events took place each year: eating too many chocolates at Christmas with my brother and sister until we fell asleep, exhausted by too much sugar, and a yearly circus. There were no animals in the circus and a few years later I understood that it was most likely a good thing.

My mother was kind enough to take me there just to see my eyes glow, and my smile. It was as if magic had uplifted my soul and all the worries in the world disappeared. I was on cloud nine and felt unstoppable.

I remember the look on my mother's face when she'd stare at me before I'd get hypnotised in the show; her eyes half filled with tears, expressing nothing but true happiness for a child that believed in magic and felt inspired by life.

The arts have always made me believe in the magic of life and the beauty of imagination, giving me space to dream, think and create; their universal language made me feel limitless. They brought moments where I felt as if I could achieve anything I set my mind to and made me believe in the impossible.

The Circus

When I was a child,
Mum took me to the circus.

Acrobats danced with the ceiling
and multicoloured ribbons -
I still remember their contortions -
freely, they lived,
travelling the world
and hypnotising us
with magic,
capturing the depth of our souls.

They wrapped the sunset in golden-glitter-dust
before the final act,
before the night would fall
in dreams.

My eyes grew wide with adoration,
as the magnetic essence fell
my imagination tore open
and drew me wings.

I grew and I flew,
just like the acrobats,
and became the dragon
of my castle.

From a young age, I became drawn to the arts and admired artists, poets and musicians across the world. I've read about different kinds of arts and different poets. The arts made me dance with solace to the flow of life with solely good intentions and that's when I knew my soul was screaming for more. I'd often go for long walks in nature and I'd dream and imagine away.

I was first an observer of the world, before the arts and nature were engraved into my soul, and the outside of my shadow. There was a town that was forty minutes drive away and, in the town, was the nearest art gallery to home. It was big enough to fit twenty people. Mum took us there twice a year, and I'd get lost between the walls while looking at paintings, decoding their meanings along with their history.

Sometimes, I'd drown into their imagery and imagined a story of my own. It was then that the foundation of my soul started to build upon art, music and poetry. The arts gave me a sense of freedom, a value of who I always had been, without never really realising it. I became enamoured with creativity through the arts and nature because they made me feel free.

That's how I fell in love with life.

The Poets

The poets are searching
for the ones that have survived,
for veteran trees
of wars and archery,
of torture and victory.

A forest
planting seeds of words
on earthy thrones,
embracing endless meanings,
defining the mother tongue
of an eternal language -
giving birth to freedom.

The flesh of their human heart
aches,
recites poetry,
their nightingale voices
eager to engrave on paper,
they bleed ink and stay quiet
while drinking
the sparkling sunset
by the lonely river.

We grieve in their absence,
celebrate in their presence,
we build roads,
they plant fields,
the invisible ones,
who are long forgotten
in ancient stories.

Visionaries in the distance:
they see in bird's-eye view
from a poet's mind,
leaving us to wonder

if

anything

precious

disappears in time

or

if our perception

is keeping us

blind.

The Painting

In a rustic art gallery,
a painting stood still
in time, in the clock
of my eyes.

It spent years,
buried
under dimming lights,
hidden afar in the make-believe city,
in a lost attic
where truthful darkness
retraces the bottom
of its timeless century.

Remaining the same as it used to be,
untold words explain the meaning
of its story.

A modern twist embracing,
seamless,
broken,
unspoken and ignored
better parts
of its forming identity,
in the flesh and the heart
of its history,
on all it ever was,
what it became,
all it is
and will ever be.

A work of art that keeps me hypnotised
behind everything I cannot see,
I am lost in its concealed
endless beauty.

Rules of Arts

I refuse to go
where there is no music,
I command instruments
to sing and yearn
for compositions
without hesitation.

I refuse to go
where there is no poetry,
I command poets to bleed
thoughts on paper
and thirst to feel human
among cascades of emotions
where four seasons flow
in the embrace of joy and sorrow,
unfolding raw performances,
spectators drown
in dream-like admiration.

I refuse to go
where there are no drawings,
I command to revive
freedom of expression
for the colours of stories
to live hereafter,
abolish silence and show us truth
in a world where art speaks to you.

Perhaps I demand nothing
except for the arts
to survive eternity
without exception,
and save us from dreaded melancholy,
leaving space for artists of all kinds
to exist, and create joy.

A heart cannot exist
in a life without rhythm,
I shall refuse to go
where a love for the arts
no longer grows.

As a young adult, I fell deep into literature. I wrote many poems but was too afraid to put myself out there. I was afraid of being judged and seen. I was terrified of speaking my truth and that remained forever in me. I was a secret writer for most of my life, keeping many pieces to myself, until I met my husband and my writing remained our secret. That's how I wanted it to be, even though he pushed me to shine in front of others. I was being me (with myself) and that's all that mattered back then. Or maybe there was an underlying wish to inspire but I didn't know how to overcome my fears of judgment. Maybe it was that I was terrified of speaking up about my talent on rooftops; something unusual, innovative and new in a world where similar thoughts ruled the planet. I felt as if I was the future living in the past and I was trying to find myself in the present.

I was a dreamer and remained in my dreams while I was wide awake. The deepest part of my soul was hidden for years, and when I began writing poetry, I felt more alive than ever.

I had awakened.

Writing helped me get through life's ups and downs, it was therapy. It helped me find myself and broke the shells of my soul that didn't belong to me.

The Ghost

The ghost of my past came to visit
in the restless night,
I was afraid of it until it dissolved
within me
then my heart remembered,
it lived in my soul,
begging to rise to the surface for years -
I thought it would die
if I'd ran from myself
though it settled in my veins.

A temporary identity loses itself
in decades
and fades from my essence
when I donate my fear to forgetfulness,
I resent the pain
from my past memories,
anxious it will fail to surrender,
frightened for the wounds
to bleed open,
aggravate,
fearful I'll suffer
twice the ache.

Though when calmness transcends
and time dissolves in numbers
to become infinite,
the spring tide of an ever-flowing waterfall
brings my heart and soul together,
they meet and sway with distress,
talk of laugher in between melodies,
follow each other's movements between
dissonance and euphony.

My mind joins the final conversation,

I become the stage of life,
I am everything I am,
no longer longing
for a false individuality
nor wondering
if the phantom exists.

The Stage

I stood
in front of the world with magnetic eyes
staring at me,
faces drawn to the stage
of emotions,
feeling the coldness of the dark,
drifting in the air
on a gloomy evening,
caressing the waves of thoughts
from heads to hearts:
the spotlight is alive,
the sun remains dead.

A vulnerable star
in acquaintance with strong faces
to sing to the silence of their music
and words,
slowly engraving
speechless applause
through still movements,
while a brave voice
awaits for the imaginary people
to listen with acceptance.

I moved out of my parents' home when I was seventeen and, when I did, I learned a lot about how to live my life the way I wanted to. I learnt the things we seldom hear about at school; how to take care of ourselves, how to take the time to reflect on who we are and embrace ourselves. Hence, I've learnt that the absence of guidance sometimes leads to independence, clarity and confusion.

I've fallen and got up again and done my best to learn from my mistakes but it was hard to fall, to try again, to fall once more, then try again. I wanted to explore a new place so I bought a one-way flight to England and moved to the UK, a place bombarded with poetry, art and music. My Uncle Freddie lived there, and he'd often tell me about painters and poets when he came to visit us in East Canada. John Constable was his favourite painter and mine, too, because his paintings exposed some of the most beautiful landscapes.

Uncle Freddie also loved reading me poems from some of the best Romantic Poets of all time, which explained my belief in heart connections growing up.

Shortly after I landed in London, I fell in love with the city. It felt like home, even when I only really had myself and poetry. Apart from Uncle Freddie, I didn't know anyone there but I had faith that I'd meet people who would become family.

I felt lost, trying to understand who I was and where I was going. I wanted to explore different career avenues and I asked myself, Why I am on this earth? What am I meant to do? What is my purpose? On rainy days, I sometimes found myself drowning in the city's loneliness and sorrows and on sunny days, its essence bloomed into a lively garden.

It's not that I questioned the value of my existence but it's that I stopped myself from flying high out of fear that too many would see me out there and that I'd fall once I'd reached the top. Because I know that not everybody can dislike you nor all love you. I felt unique and different from the majority.

My soul knew I wanted to be a writer but the uncertainty and rejection felt hopeless at times, and I was afraid it wouldn't get me anywhere and that it would bring me back to the beginning of everything one day, over and over again.

Then I asked myself again, what I truly wanted, and it was to inspire people through words. To touch as many souls and hearts as I could.

To tell others not to live in fear, to dream big, create, to raise their voice and expose their talents, but first, I knew I had to do these things myself and lead by example. I wanted to be an author but, often, when I thought about sharing my work, I felt so nervous that I wanted to vomit and tear my heart apart. I was terrified of not being good enough.

I started teaching children for a while, and a new kind of love fell upon me. It was the love of teaching kindness, thoughtfulness, self-awareness, resilience, independence and confidence. A love for sharing wisdom and knowledge, transforming them into treasure boxes. I wanted to teach them the power of nature, music, art, literature, self-love and mysteries from ancient wisdom. I hope that I'd be, in my turn, a teacher to remember, like I remembered some of my teachers for making a difference in my life, without them really kno wing it. And it was their kind hearts that made all the difference.

However, nothing was as strong as the love I felt for poetry.

Perhaps, it wasn't love at all, it was a thousand times more powerful than that.

Writing always helped me conquer my broken heart. It was part of who I was going to be for ever and writing liberated me to the core of my soul.

*It felt as if I'd found true love, except that I not only wanted it, I **needed** it in my life.*

Searching for my Soul

I went searching for gold in a cave,
hoping to find the yolk of the sun
in a new colour
to brighten my way
to a light-hearted daffodil sky.

I wanted to drown
my insanity
in a sinking boat,
travelling the ocean,
caught up in a shark's cage -
in a film put on pause.

The fainted clouds disappeared
in chaos
as if splashes of paint spilled
over my body and rationality
to cover the bruises
of my missing dignity.

Thoughtless promises anchored
on my skin
transforming into dust,
dissolving in the imaginary.

The wind stood still,
the earth became the moon,
fearful of rising freely,
contemplating the image of air,
breathing in existence
while time distills
in an hourglass,
measured by sugar spoons.
I am looking for the underlying truth of myself,

for a feather to take me
surfing on stars
that hide on starry nights,
for the flesh of my turmoil to embrace
the journey,
for light to chase shadows
to illuminate the inner me,
yet I am in a pitch-black cave
and my darkness is dazzling
as sunlight.

The Forgotten

In fourth grade, I searched for a place
to visit,
in Geography class through the pages
of an atlas.

I learnt about the oceans and seas
and how a passport could set me free,
dreamt of flying beyond limits
to become who I was born to be.

Though the thoughts of the world may be too broad
for me to explore,
the ones I carry never cease,
are never ignored.

Searching for my soul
was my toilsome discovery,
I fought like a warrior with a shield
in the storms of the sea,
sailed broken ships
and struggled to build confidence
through my unknown skills
to conquer insecurities in my head.

Intended actions,
the heart of my ambitions,
the life I live is yet to be written,
by no one other than myself,
travelling within me,
the best lessons learned
make you feel beyond
what you can see.

One opens a blank book

and words of the heart
unfold a story that is yet to begin living.

They taught me at school
to cherish knowledge
and use it as a tool,
though I remember,
one class has been long forgotten.

Teaching from the Heart

Good morning,
little darlings,
the charm of her voice softly speaks.
Her smile greets the children
as she is resting the tears
that kept the night awake,
her courage singing words
of beautiful daily beginnings.

Her aura
moves the children by inviting them
to dance in imagination,
she's an ever-growing flower,
carrying the scent of lavender's perfum.
The warmth of her arms
holds a love for emotions,
where the teardrops find consolation.

Her kind nature caresses all
cries and helps to surrender,
she puts bandages on a child's sorrows,
turning them into nostalgic memories
as their voices grow.

In her soul, absent is the duty,
though a choice to empower
health of the mind,
heart and body.

She makes every child feel as they matter,
inspires them to blossom,
to aim high, above the sky,
to shine as bright as the sun,
to perform in their own way,
like the unique star each one is.

Shaping our future leaders,
she is a teacher I remembered.

Dancing with Poetry

I am no lonely soul -
but when I am alone
I pour my heart out
and set it free -
the flesh of my emotions
submerges to the beat
of my company.

I fall in dreams,
wide awake,
lovingly holding
profound silence within me.

I immerse in words,
capturing their sounds,
my mind gracefully unfolding
a sweet melody,
singing rhymes
with pure simplicity.

On nights like these I fall in love,
under the starlight,
and dance in my living room
with poetry.

During the cherry blossom season, I met my husband at a music festival in Brighton. We were different, but agreed on what mattered the most; we'd grow wiser together by learning from each other. It was the soul kind of love, the one that overcomes death.

At the beginning, we took things slow and got to know each other. This created a solid foundation for our relationship. We trusted each other.

His upbringing was very different from mine. Our personalities were almost opposites, but differences complemented each other's strengths and weaknesses and our love turned into lifetimes.

We had one child, Heloise, who taught me the unique kind of love a mother can offer. When she was a baby, I held her in my arms while she'd fall asleep. Holding her against my chest, I could feel her heart beating against my stomach. Her eyes closed, she looked as if she was at peace with herself. And I thought to myself, can you sleep in my arms for the rest of time? Though, I knew I asked for the impossible and I didn't mean my words because seeing a child grow is one of the most organic and most pure beautiful aspects of life, through a mother's eyes. The story of her life is yet to be shared, it will be shared when the time feels right.

My daughter had a beautiful niece, Emily, who reminded me of myself. She was an endless dreamer of the world and her youthful pride made me believe in the impossible. I felt so lucky for sharing my life with such an imperfectly perfect family.

When my memory started slipping through time with age, music and poetry helped me conquer forgetfulness. The arts are often my salvation and I thank my family - along with nature - for remaining patient with me.

My Husband

My husband is sitting in the rocking chair
on the porch
after years of oak trees.

The smell of freshly cut grass
tingles his nose in the noon-day sun
each summer.

It is a long time since he could hear
the sound of wind,
the sky is clear,
the air is crisp,
his breath is deep.

We left behind a house filled with space,
for endless conversations,
hidden treasures
that only had meaning for us:
a home full of character and tenacity,
together we built the story
of our destiny.

I used to paint in the attic,
write until dawn near the fireplace
by the comfort of a cup of peppermint tea,
play piano at sunset,
by the window overlooking the sea,
he was into acoustics
and loved reading philosophy.

Wrinkled hands yet youthful eyes,
pieces of our soul always remain in us.

Still, when time comes to forget,
temporarily,

the lukewarm thunder will awake our wind-chime
and make it dance until it breaks.

Until then, say goodbye, we must,
and disappear in dust
until we meet again,
when recognised cadence is reborn
for us to remember,
and welcome a new love story
to surrender.

By the Sea

Burning shadows and innocent words
on the coldest night by the low-lit sea,
my tongue spoke the language of anger,
your lips whispered storms of exasperation,
meaningless lies
unfolding truths.

We both stood soul to soul in disagreement,
still, we love each other too much
not to forgive and let forget
from night to morning,
endlessly.

A Child's Touch

For my daughter

Her feet are as big as the palms of my hands,
this tiny life born in the love of my arms,
her eyes smiling back at me
because she knows more than myself -
her beautiful being
will change my darkness into light.

And she's the sound of every heartbeat
that keeps my love alive.

That Feeling

Holding you in my arms
while you fall asleep
is so meaningful,
it feels as if I'm holding everything beautiful
in this world
all at once.

Family Children

When the little people are around me,
my worries don't stand a chance:
funny laughs and cheeky smiles -
when the little people tell a joke,
the sun and rain reconcile.

Enchanting voices and pretty blue eyes,
when the little people look at me
trouble stops growing in my garden
and tulips rise.

Vast imagination and minds full of solutions,
when the little people fear I am in danger
they send dragons to fly and conquer.

Small jeans and holly dresses,
when the little people are with me
I always look my best.

Big genuine hearts and the sweetest touch,
when the little people see my flaws
they love me just as much.

Little people do not stay so little,
someday, taller than me they'll be
but to me little people they will always be!

Little Darling

For my niece

My little darling,
why are you still up at this time of night?
Are you caught up in your dreams
or are you battling against your fight?

This day can never be long enough,
when you are drowning into your love,
you've held your chin so high,
I forgotten you could still cry.

If city lights could stay in the dark,
for as long as you would like them to,
would you stop sleeping and stay awake,
from one end of the world to the other?

If candlelight could replace the black
of your bedroom,
would you let the stars run away
or let them settle in your pillow?

If the sunrise disappears on you in the morning
would you let it go?
Or would you search for it until you found it again?

My little darling,
it's time to fall asleep,
and awake, ready
to live your wildest dreams.

When Music Speaks

(A night I remember very well)

It is quite some time, more like years, since I was in Paris last.
This evening, I'm on top of the world with my husband, holding hands as if we were thirty-three and newly in love. It's as if we've travelled back in time, except for our wrinkled skin which remains evergreen on the inside. The city lights hypnotise me in their darkness and romantic dreams; we are wrapped in gold by the Eiffel Tower and it feels magical, the *kind of magic in which acrobats dance with ceilings and ribbons.*
I've forgotten my camera. I've left it at our hotel in the heart of the city, so I capture this evening with my mind and engrave it in the pocket of my dearest memories.

I could stay here for hours, embracing the moment and listening to music. Ah, the music. I love listening to it speak. 'River Flows' starts playing, and it transforms me into a piano. The wind flies through my thoughts and I am now holding the remembrance of my second heart, my gut, over my head.

The sweetness of the melody takes me back to my living room, where I spent countless nights writing poetry by the fireplace in the comfort of my broadest imagination, surrounded by low-lit candles alongside the lasting scent of fresh lilies of the valley.

Through the window, the skyscraper lights of London are too far to see and are obscured by a view of painted oak trees, clouds and sky, coloured by the Caribbean sea. I'm comfortably tucked in a corner of England and my soul is always ready to write on nights, with a side of peppermint tea, when the moon shines bright. On a starry night, I look at the stars and look for constellations, and I wonder if the rest of the world look for them, too.

I sit at the wooden desk I bought more than fifteen years ago from a second-hand furniture shop near Archway Station. Next to it stands my piano, patiently waiting to be heard. It took me years to learn how to play, because my poetic nature kept interrupting me by writing words for endearing, unfinished pieces.
But, gosh, those poetry books turned out amazingly. They warmed up like sweet apple pies on a crisp autumn day and baked perfectly four summers later.

They were so ready to embrace my fingers as they touched the piano keys and each word sang along with feeling.

When my niece began singing lessons, she was there to accompany the music, my thousand phrases and the softness of my voice. She had the perfect pitch range from the sound of a tuba to a woman's voice to a violin and a piccolo. She was, herself, the missing instrument that glued this small moving 'band' together, like the beat of drums holding the heartbeat of a song. But, oh, we danced to our own beat, just the way we liked it.

There was one evening when we spent hours practising 'Hey Jude' by The Beatles. Ah, this song! I was in my early adult years when this song was in the mainstream and it soon became a number one hit across the globe. I was lost in life, searching for my career and what made me feel alive the most, learning about the world and becoming the person I wanted to be, chasing my dreams as if I was running to catch a plane or a kite flying in the sky at Hampstead Heath park.

This song inspired me to sing sad songs aloud many times when I was home alone, dancing in the kitchen while cooking fresh fish, broccoli and mashed potatoes and it made things better, as I expressed my emotions to my absent audience.

I was brave, you know, *not waiting for someone to perform with*, I was taking the risk of the neighbours hearing me scream the silent voice that had lived inside of me for too long. And gosh, I began to feel better. But then there was this guy who was a little older than me, whom I met at the fish market on a Sunday. He was quite a man, but his attitude quickly grew into a boy's after our first kiss. It felt as if I was in love for the first time, his blue eyes were magnetic, but then he disappeared after three dates at the drive-in. I cried for a few nights until his essence fell on me and knocked my love glasses, and then I knew the distance was good for me, so I joined my friends for an evening at Greenwich Park. They brought their guitars, and we danced among the veteran trees in our light blue, straight cut jeans and hippie tops while they sang The Beatles songs. And, finally, there was the light, the summer sunset, appearing over my rainy cheeks. Grapes and cheese picnics with glasses of strawberry wine. We were thirsty for dancing. We acted like a bunch of kids who ate two chocolate bars in a row before going to bed and looked a bit like fools pretending to be birds as our arms and pirouettes were aiming for the sky, but it was fun and it made us laugh. Gosh, how I felt so much better and fell in love with the picture of that night, along with the following ones.

I suddenly bring myself back to Paris as 'It's My Life' by Bon Jovi starts to play. It's been quite a ride since we were here last. It's a beautiful evening. My husband puts his arm around me, and a younger couple next to us tells us how cute we are, us elderly people looking so in love after many years of shipwreck, perseverance, blossoming gardens and true love. They looked cute, too, these two, who kept on debating about where to go next for a drink.

A new song begins to play. My husband and I once danced on this floor of the Eiffel Tower. He takes me in his arms and we dance again for a minute or two as I place my head on his beating heart. And he whispers out loud, Honey, your soul can never grow old; it's evergreen. Oh, how I love this man. The song skips to a country song I have never heard before, and I 'remember when' I put the camera in his backpack before leaving.

Ah, music! I love the beauty it brings into my world. But what I adore about music, oh, what I love the most, is how it makes me remember and how it makes me feel, in the present.

Here I sit in this quiet cafe by the river, admiring the view and taking in the music, now yearning to go home to play 'River Flows' with the note sheets inked in the sound of my memory.

GrandPa's Story

My wife and I had different upbringings but they both taught us a lot and would lead us to the adults that'd we become.

For me, my childhood was mostly about surviving, surrendering, and overcoming the trauma of events I wish I'd never seen. It wasn't a choice, to decide in which country I'd be born into, nor in which century. It wasn't the kind of fame I'd hoped for back then, as I was once told people from other corners of the world knew about us from the media. How much did they understand?

Some moments of my youth broke my heart, though not my future. We moved from one place to another, carrying bundles of hope, hoping we'd found a place of protection. Still, I remember a life of tranquillity before the roars of the battlefields began. It was near that time when I wondered if I was destined to die of fear at such a young age. Some of my past feels too painful to talk about and when I think about it, sometimes, I feel as if a bullet is attacking my gut.

Some of the places where I have been, created wounds that I'm still trying to heal after years, so I'd like for the locations to remain vague when I tell my story. Though we weren't far from Britain.

Have you ever enjoyed a special moment with someone special and looked at them, hoping that present would never end, so you took a mental picture? I had the opposite feelings at times where traumatic photographs never really faded from my memory.

It was a very warm day, I remember it well, when I thought I'd never see my mother again and that emotional scar lived within me for years. I looked at my father and thought, he looked like a man of despair.

That day crushed parts of my soul. It almost killed me yet the most painful part was that I remained alive. It's as if the world became obscured and I was covered in blood, though I was not.

The battle felt so long and my fearful father's voice echoed in my head for the next few nights. I'll find you again, may this hell not harm her, he screamed, repeatedly.

My father once told me that he'd get me an orange slide, so I could play without worry, as I should have been as a child. He once wrote his anger on paper, one of the stories he tells best, 'Orange Slide'.

Orange Slide

My father's words.

I hid behind the tallest tree I could see,
escaping the sun
that was burning my shoulders,
my weary shirt couldn't cover
the rough hands of a man
that lost every part of his masculinity,
I touch the dripping sweat on the back
of my son,
alongside misery, it engraves despair
in my hands.

I want to lick the dirt off them
as I've not drunk water in thirty-two hours
and my throat is thirsty for surviving,
the earth is dry and I'm patiently waiting
for the rain,
like a single piece of uncoloured grass
in a field as wide as the sky.

Every bone in my body is weak,
becoming softer than a dying eagle's feathers
which has stopped flying for days or weeks,
as he's been captured
and put in a cage.

If I could simply become an ocean
and feed water to my own child,
but with a small miracle,
my reality could transform into me
drinking half a glass of water.
I heard heavy bullets in the depth of the day,
buzzing in my ears like the chorus
of the song 'The End of Us',
they took me away

while I carried my son in my arms,
squeezing him hard like a snake
afraid to lose his prey,
and there we sat in the back of an old dark van
looking through the glass window,
that I punched twice with my bleeding knuckles
as I see my wife wearing her faded white dress
that's ripped apart,
blood on her legs,
dripping from her womankind,
no protection,
if only that were the least of our worries,
she is running barefoot on the rocky, dirty pavement,
tears sliding down her cheeks.

She tries to smile, hopelessly hoping
our world won't split apart,
in the belief we will see each other again,
she is the mirror of my son
who fell asleep on my knees
so I covered his dignity with my eyes
so he can't see
because I don't want to cause him any more pain
by forcing him to say goodbye
to the woman who gave him life
with barely anything other than love,
organs and blood.

I think it was a boat that took us, but I'm still not sure,
we both passed out in the heat
so I can't remember clearly,
we are now in our new home
without a bedroom or a kitchen,
close to the kind of places I've always known:
a rooftop and warm blankets so I won't die
from the cold at night
and my body heat will warm up my son,
the only gesture I have left

as a living man, who's transforming into a boy
by providing a bare minimum for his family.

In the burning sun,
I left the other half of me,
we try to find our place in this world,
along with all the others like us -
as I know what that really means -
but even if I'd found our happiness,
we wouldn't be able to stay,
my son and I,
in the comfort of an abandoned wooden shed
in a dead forest where animals come
to fill their empty stomachs.

People I don't know,
but who claim to be on our side,
asked me to show fear and to justify
the terror that appears in my straight face -
how can they not see it?
When did I become so disfigured
that I can barely recognise myself?

I woke up in the morning,
scratching my stomach from the bedbugs
stuck in the rigid mattress,
I had been hungry for so long,
I threw up on the floor
as I swallowed
the first juicy piece of my pineapple.

My son is finally getting stitches,
I'm just glad he's alive
even though he may feel
as if his heart is on fire,
maybe that's how it feels
when you die slowly,

and you really want to live
and feel intensely at the same time,
despite the physical
and emotional pain
that takes complete control of who you are
as if you are lying on a bed
in a mental institution
in the 1930's,
that became your permanent home.

You have an unplanned and uncertain life
in front of you
but when you are seven years old, like my son,
and stuck in a television drama,
in which they show your open story on the news
of hopeless watchers
who see us
without doing anything at all,
it's like spitting on my tongue and rinsing it away
with salty vinegar afterwards,
as I know what that tastes like.

This is not the kind of life I intended to give
my son
when I built him with my organ and pure love
on the night I met his mother,
I am a madman for wanting to fight
for the rights of being human
just like the ones who have to fight
for the rights of buying alcohol
after drinking too much,
or the ones who fight for the last piece of chicken
when they have a full buffet on the table.
They have saved us, and we are now breathing
more easily in injustice
and I can't help counting the days
until when I'll see the end of it

as I can't stand on my two feet properly
if I don't have all of my toes.

How can I find myself when I lost almost everything
I owned, including a piece of my mind
and the only romantic love I've ever known?
How can I justify myself when they already put a face
on my skin that isn't my own?
Can you let me choose my own eyebrows, mouth,
ears, eyes, nose and future?
Or at least bring me back my wife and give my son
what he deserves:
a happy life
in which all he needs to worry about
is where to find a playground
with a bright orange slide.

We lived in a place between borders for a while, it felt as if the ocean was our home. What we longed for most was freedom, and I thought to myself, in what world could innocent people not be free?

We had no choice but to learn how to overcome life's challenges when we could escape and detach from the dilemmas of the world. After the deportation, we were searching for quite some time for a place to belong.

During this time, my father taught me the value of nature and the universe, how to cherish it and learn from it. As a farmer, he often looked at the stars for answers but I seldom did. Not because I didn't believe in them but because I didn't really understand them, and their way of life. Though, I could listen to him for hours without getting bored and admired the glow of the moon whenever I could see it. Farmers often relied on the Harvest moon in the fall. It brought us light during the nights and indicated the beginning of a new season.

I knew that meant changes and a new surrounding.

Borders

If battles of sorrows tear you apart,
if the storm takes your home abroad,
freedom gives you the only choice:
to surrender.

When success counts failures,
when hearts filled wide with fear
carry on living
in nightmares of foreign affairs,
dreams,
the restless mind,
hopeful for peace
that once vanished,
may find us again.

If a change of unpredicted plan resonates
at peals of thunder,
if the roads diverge into a maze,
searching for bravery on the land
by following the moon's glowing hope,
may one be set free,
losing confusion becomes my salvation
though at times I wonder if the exits do exist.

The escape of a forbidden love for liberation
between transparent borders and broad open gates,
the disappearance of constant battles,
alongside daunting fights,
the allowance of loud speeches when one is too weak
to speak,
we built our strength from the bottom
of our vulnerability,
walked uncertain roads to find a refugee.
Combats of the borders,
so long.
so familiar.

A World of Fear

The noise of the world screams
on bare roofs, like fireworks
disrupting a placid midnight sky
eager to rest in silence.

Inviting pain to enter my mind,
the hurt settling in my heart,
in hopes the flesh of my peace retains,
though I once saw a child
rock his father to death -
I wish these memories,
my eyes, could forget.

A journey that took me far
from what a childhood's remembrance should have been,
the war was near, born at my door,
seven years of my life I lived as a child,
met with fireflies that came to play
to erase darkness and shine bright
in my hopeful dreams,
one night they disappeared,
and all left to do was to conquer,
create light
with the darkly sun
reflecting on an abandoned armour,
under its warmth,
my soul burnt
soon to be lost letters,
once written with the last of my strength.

Wandering thoughts interrupting
inner peace,
my heavy heart begged to stay strong,
even if all seemed to have gone wrong.

The Art of Wisdom

From day to day I would wonder
if I'd breathe comfortably tomorrow
in a place meant to feel like home,
or if one could bloom in a world of fear,
where all flowers are now hoping
for rain drops to nourish them again,
instead of making them drown,
after the storm passes.

Living for the Harvest Moon

I don't recall how old I was but it was at a time when I didn't count birthdays, none of them, for myself or anyone. Time didn't seem to exist. Or perhaps, it did, but it didn't seem to matter or make a difference in the big picture of life. I couldn't keep track of what day it was but I had noticed the natural world would whisper the season's glow to my eyes. It was a full circle on repeat where red, yellow and orange leaves would fall on my head then be abandoned for mild snow to settle every so often. Then, blossoming hearts and trees would meet the extreme warm weather.

I lived in a seasonless world where changes were big enough but seldom had solid meanings. The earth often seemed to move slowly for decades, then it felt as if a tornado had hit everything we had built for years, with the broken pieces of ourselves.

The storms were invisible but they would often give me an upset stomach, leaving me half-fainted and not hungry for days. Our place was as delicate as a lonely feather that drifted from its nest, hoping to find its mother hen. I didn't like talking about specific places back then because I was often confused about where I was a lot of the times, and where I'd stay.

I didn't care for the most comfortable bed, nor the cleanest kitchen, I just wanted someting to rest on and a place where I'd find food. My body was eager for protection, water, and gardens filled with vegetables. I felt I did not need much, but the rest of me was craving for inner peace, and to feel alive.

The fear of the unknown kept me awake many nights. My mind was agitated for hours, dreaming about an escape plan as well as what other spots on Earth might look like. I wondered if some also drank the rain or the snow when there was no other options or used leaves as bed mattresses or banana peels as plates, but then I also imagined and thought about what 'more' looked like. Maybe some had luxurious beds made of *wishing stars*.

The sunset's glory was worth a roofless house and the sky was my father's favourite topic to talk about since I was a child. The rain would sometimes sweep our tears away and the mystery of the universe was our salvation, along with entertainment. We'd spend endless nights gazing at the stars, trying to read constellations.

It was seldom easy for me to do. I was only good at reading words, people and distant tornados.

My father had told me that before he met my mother, and our part of the world collapsed a little, he was a farmer.

He loved talking about the past, it brought him everyday comfort. The moons would tell him about leaf growth and they'd spend hours talking about the future. Nature didn't speak too much but was always a *patient listener*. The light of the Harvest Moon had remained his favourite throughout the years. He once told me, that to him, it represented progress in eternity. Back then, during the September or October Harvest Moon, it meant that we'd try to break free and move somewhere distant where we could find a better shelter.

It was a night of the Harvest Moon when we had planned to escape but, before leaving, my father asked me to write a letter to my mother so that she'd know where we were going. And so I did and let it fly in the wind but I was hopeful that she wouldn't forget our pact; my mother had once told me that if we'd get lost or separated, we'd return where we came from in the very first place and I hoped we would, if we had the chance.

My dream was to return to my childhood house, even though it would never be as homely as it used to be. I begged the stars we'd find each other again but it was on that faithful night we left, hoping the moonlight would lead us somewhere good.

We finally found a safe place to stay for a while, and the madness of the world had quietened down. I started feeling peace and living differently, wondering if the people I met along the way found a place for their weaknesses and strengths to survive, and if anybody else felt like they'd been hiding in a cave or lost forest for years but mostly I wondered if my mother would ever come back to us. I didn't say goodbye. I don't say goodbye to my family, I had hoped we'd find each other again. I knew she'd think of us every day and it had been a very long time since I had seen her smile. I wondered where she had gone and if the sky could lead her home, but then I thought,

where does the sky end?

Fallen with the Night

I've fallen with the night,
burned my fatigue through a candle light,
the smell of the stars never felt so bright,
making me sneeze my way out of misery.

There was a murder,
stardust killed my anger,
and the rest remain mysterious.

I lie on a cold bed of leaves,
wishing to never see the day again,
if only time could restrain the rain
from pouring,
the shell of my soul
could turn into sunlight
and allow a child to bloom.

I was once in nameless wars,
forgotten in world history,
shed tears of blood on pavements,
questioning my identity,
dreaming in contradictions, sharing the pain
of my missing royalty.

I owed soldiers no less than immense loyalty
between the thoughts in my head and reality,
I paid to live in the clouds now and then,
to disappear in the crowd.

Then, I try to rest, awake,
while the world goes asleep
and I -
I am screeching
from the inside,

loud and wild
to wake all others. They sacrifice sleep,
to protect themselves
from the sounds of battlefields
at night
as fearfulness lies next to them.

Year Unknown

It's 1957,
a Sunday,
I think,
I am not too sure,
whispers the absence of time.

My timekeeper lives two towns away
between woodpeckers and corner shops
and disappears in the darkened sun.

Full moon cycles repeat themselves,
changing the shades of darkness
or they remain silent,
unnoticed.

Into the woods,
I live,
it's 1957
or perhaps before or after.

I am not too sure,
though what I know
is that the war is over.

There were years of moving to different places, searching for a place for our minds, hearts and bodies to settle. The confusion and uncertainty interrupted my optimism and hopes at times. There became only one place left to go, back to where we had come from, as I once told my mother I'd return if I'd get lost. Back to the beginning, though I knew it would never be as harmonious and as quiet as it was when I was a young child, a place which had once felt safe and far from the chaos of the world.

It was a sombre evening when we arrived at the place of my shortened childhood. I opened the half-broken, maroon wooden door and it's as if my heart stopped for a split-second.

There she was, lying on the sofa looking weak, hungry and as if she hadn't slept in decades. She was wearing an old forest-green dress, covered with mud but there was no blood. Her bones embraced the shape of her face, her body floating in that dress yet she was alive and, astonishingly smiling.

My mother.

We stayed together for a few years, out of love and out of fear we'd get separated again. Though, as the years past, I urged for freedom and new scenery. So, I left my parents in a safe place with a guilty heart, knowing with the changing times that I'd be back only to visit, and carved a new path. I knew, in their turn, once ready to let go of fear and ready to build new memories, they'd would move somewhere new, too.

A Man of Feeling

I once heard that time heals all wounds, but does it remain truthful when I have a wound that's bleeding a river from my knee?

I remember a day when my mother was a nurse and gently wrapped me in tears and bandages, sweeping the sound of my troubles away. She was a brave woman who carried multi-layered emotions and professions all at once.

We lived in a wooden house wrapped around trees where we'd admire the sky's beauty on dark days, tucked away from the big city. Our pathway was detached from the majority, and we'd rarely drive by the opinions of the world.

The front porch was always quiet. It was fragile and would always let in heavy rain, and it was strong enough to stop the door from *breaking in pain*. Our living room had French windows, a fire-place and a small wooden oak desk Dad had made with his bare hands. He was a creative man and his deep love for trees was contradictory; he'd spent long days spilling ink on blank pages, filling the house with music lyrics, and countless mornings planting trees so we'd never run out. He had a natural talent; his lyrics were the lullabies I'd hear before going to bed when I was a child.

I loved poetry and music lyrics for most of my life before I even met my wife, who is poetry itself. They were more than enough to make me dream away.

The living room was the best place in the house to go when we'd hear bullet noise far away and fear would never stay together as a family every time, but we were also more than that; it was having the choice of wanting well for one another.

When I was five and brave enough to be one of the men of the house by chopping wood around seven in the morning, so we could be protected from the cold during winter, I saw each season long coming in front of me. They didn't mean anything to me because I'd wonder over and over again if I'd be able to get out of here one day without doubts, and explore new patterns. I felt it within me that I was, at once, a soldier and a traveller at heart, solely because I felt lost among the misery, happiness and treasured viewless beauties of this natural sight that surrounded me.

Sometimes, late at night, Mum and Dad would light candles on the kitchen table, and we'd spread out puzzles of different places and drink lukewarm apple tea to get more comfortable in our skins, letting the blood flow freely through our veins.
We had all of the happiness in the world.

The walls in my room were a comforting pale blue, but the paint began fading after years of ignorance and low-maintenance. There was a painting in my closet that I never understood. It lived there, left contemplating by itself. No one knew where it had come from. When the night tumbled upon us, I'd cover my ears with my pillows before falling asleep and lose myself in a book of adventure, after Dad's lullabies. I'd choose a book from my parents' bedroom library. There were a selection of books that were undated, and they'd tell me bedtime stories about people who'd once existed in the world, the places they'd been to and the landscapes they had once found. They helped me escape from the external madness that sometimes shot drastic thoughts through our minds. I'd forget what I wanted to forget. We had it all for quite some time.

Then, one morning, I woke up, years in the future, and the earth screamed dreadful silence. It had been a while since we were reunited with these emotions as a family, since the drama of the past. It was the day we'd waited for, for a very long time, without counting the days, one we'd thought we'd never see. And there it was, sitting on the steps of our front porch: *peace.*

Mum and Dad knew what that meant for me, imprisoned in sorrow and wanting more because I knew they'd now be okay without me, and without questions, they let me go with the confidence they'd see me again. There was no doubt that this modern world would never run out of pens and paper, tea, trees, boats and mysteries of life. There would be more of the things that are needed and the ones that are not. But in the matters of the heart, my body content was displaced and I had an urge to discover all that I didn't know, and to roam by choice. The truth is that I no longer knew how to live a settled nor still life, and was yearning to find a place I'd never dreamt of leaving; my childhood house wasn't it. And, even though family was important to me, I knew the world offered beautiful destinations, despite the chaos that also lives within it.

I left on an afternoon when the winter sun was the light of my unknown plans. I made my way to France and took a boat to my destiny, but was my first destination Jupiter or Saturn: I couldn't decide. Perhaps, it is places that change with how I see the rest of the world, if any of it is no illusion, that I am yet to know. If I am miles away from Earth, can my distance change who I am?

I didn't have enough space to think, and it was killing me. It could take me months or years to get to where I'd like to be and get across the moon by gaining guidance from the stars. I was fighting against time, for the first decade in history. Shall I focus on the present? Can I question if I am immortal or if I'll have to return in another lifetime? Or is the flesh of my soul living in eternal youth? I am searching in darkness for the underlying light of myself, and a sense of belonging where freedom rules kingdoms and forgotten villages too small to appear on a map of the world. And, suddenly, I stand tall and ask myself: which forest have I outgrown? Was it a forest or something else?

Back where I used to live, in my childhood, I once dreamt about visiting all the countries and planets, and learning how to build a boat through imagination so that I could avoid swimming in cold oceans because, after months, it got tiring. *It's tiring, to live it all at once, to be a bird and a fish at the same time* and to dance in the storms on a boat but, beyond it all, I learn the *knowledge of the sea.* I am a hopeless wanderer and optimistically hope that my instinct will lead me to the right shore. It's not the thunder or the rain I'm afraid of (because the sound of their music moves me, in some kind of directions that get lost in translation), it's the solitude that attacks me when I'm temporarily disoriented, and it feels as if I'll never get rid of it because I wonder why it's here, why it came and if it will grow. I never cease to rage with it and find solace by crying my way out of melancholy.

I fall at sea and in love over and over again when my sun comes out of affliction, and its light is astonishing. Its brilliance takes me to a newfound deserted island with many mountains and rivers. The land appears like a painting from the seventeenth century; it's dark and speaks of silence and music. Emotions take the lead, and dead trees come alive and, beneath creativity, I can see what this place once was and what it became. It takes me far from the drama and gossip of the rest of the world, and all I can hear are the waves of the sea and the hummingbirds singing.

The natural world teaches me, loneliness does not always remain my enemy.

After sailing and walking for hours, I came across a small, abandoned vegetable garden next to a vintage, grey wooden cabin on a small island. I sit in the shade on a three-foot-high hammock, even if I'm afraid it may split in two. I open my backpack and find the love of my life, *my notebook*. And I talk to myself while my unruly thoughts flip through the pages of this small precious diamond, among the things I call wealth. I am deeply concerned that concrete cannot meet my heart with worldly matters when I've been taught to grow tomatoes and plant more trees than plastic and coins. I grasp the wind as it comes, and then I disappear with it. I am a ghost in time and become a plane and fly from one place to another until I find what I'm looking for, *a place to be*. Despite these escapades which seem endless, I do not stop, and I keep going back to the present, future and sometimes drop into the past.

With my heart's ink, I anchored my name in the United Kingdom. In January, year unknown, I drank two bottles of wine on the still boat and got sea sick.

The next morning, I'd forgotten my past regrets and it wasn't the end of the world after all, but it was close as I could still feel the alcohol in my blood the next afternoon. I am a man of integrity, and I surrender occasional drunken days and nights, but I do not live to forget - **I live a life to remember** (*not where I have been but what I have learned, and what I am learning about the world and myself*). Then, I move on to new wisdom and transport my baggage on strangers' roads.

Before the end of the borders, I met a man who insisted on talking about his way of life. He told me a story about the power of stones and how the sea always managed their delivery. It was the beauty of their appearance; their mauve or green colour and their glimmering glaze with empty meanings. We spent two hours walking along the coast, trying to find perfect stones and welcomed the sunset and his grandson before the dark. It was time for me to go and I had to leave the stones as they were too heavy: I told myself there would be some more, somewhere in the United Kingdom and I went searching for some stones upon my arrival, but I didn't have to go far. I ended up in London, England at a hotel near Southbank by the River Thames. It becomes the entertainment of hundreds of people in afternoons, so it's not the place for me to settle in for too long.

But it doesn't mean that I don't want to stay for quite some time and enjoy morning breakfast with a view which involves flowers, pear trees and the city. All through the month of June, I sat at a classy white table by the window, before the chaos of the day, and there was seldom anybody to see through the window so I could embrace the mesmerizing setting. On my last day, I took a picture and stored it somewhere in my head, hoping it would remain in my memory. My hands were left bare with gratitude; I am richer on the inside because I hold nothing but the clothes I am wearing and lessons to fight against danger because there are mythical dragons and dungeons in this world we live in.

I am a warrior filled with innocence, and restless during the nights, carrying the puzzle pieces I used to hold by memory to find somewhere to go, hoping to land on my two feet.

I surf over shallow waters, and that has made all the difference in all of my actions. *I am searching for the right place to become everlasting, and I let my feet lead me to where I do not know where I am going.* I seek a sense of belonging. And I must not stop until I find what I am looking for because I will find it.

I seek hope, happiness and truth with who I am and where I'm meant to go. *I am a man of feeling, a man that speaks from his mind but acts from the heart,* and whose passport is filled with messy quill ink, music notes and lyrics, surviving blood and countless footsteps. I have it all, I always had everything, but here I am still left wondering: what is a home?
Is it a feeling?

I settled in England, a place that gave 'home' a sense of truth and meaning. Finding a place where I could live in calmness felt as if a bullet had been taken out of my back. A few years back, the thought of surrendering and settling in freedom, calmness, passion and happiness felt impossible, and it felt surreal at times to believe that *I did come out from such a deep darkness* I once thought I'd never escape. From then on, I believed anything was possible and it broke my heart to see others live out of fear, a feeling that seemed anchored in my wife's mind at times, although it seems to be a common thing for a lot of us, despite we go through. I had hope she wouldn't live in it for long.

My childhood taught me to care for myself as well as for others. In London, I developed an interest in medicine and music. Music, a prescription for the soul that helps people heal sadness, process emotions, forget physical pain and helps people to unwind. I found a second-hand acoustic guitar at a shop tucked away from the city, and played as I had played for lifetimes. I played in hospitals for 'patients'. Hence, I prefer to say, for uncles, mothers, children, musicians, lawyers, singers, along with all of the other people who lived there for some time.

England is a place where my musical talent made me feel valued and gave me the chance to connect with many incredible artists, and I became a part of them. People wanted me there, so I stayed. I settled. *I wanted nothing more than to stay.* Home.

I met my wife at a music festival in Brighton and our initial meeting was chaotic because we were almost opposite from each other but we agreed to do our best and take the time to understand each other, which changed everything for the better. After the evening we met, we met again in London the next evening and sat near the Thames and it felt as if we lived that moment before. She had a pure essence, and a pure heart of gold, which I always thought was a rare thing to find in the world. I fell in love with the softness and kindness of her soul and I knew that was long-lasting. I was only lucky her soul reflected in her outside beauty. Her soul embellished with time but I knew, as beautiful as she was, a youthful appearance didn't grow in reverse.

Hence, our wrinkles are the scars of our survival and there is something beautiful in that, too.

Heart Country

I am at war with my heart country,
fighting for my rights:
not as genuine -
not as a person -
though as a number
and an object.

I am harmless in the lawful battle
of directions and doubts,
n my eyes,
my notebook unfolds
the work progress of obedience.

I build and follow my steps,
in stones I create walls
for my protest,
I declare my value
and soldiers agree:
a pure and precious existence,
the purest gold on Earth.

Proving myself persistently,
read my number
by the name
of my full identity,
look closely and see me
move forward
Rights too far ahead to see,
could a kingdom help me fight my way
to victory?

I am fighting for my rights,
not as a number -

not as an object -
but as genuine,
and as a person.

Set me free and let me be,
that is how I end war
with my heart country.

I Haven't Smiled in a Hundred Years

Leaving behind a story
where pain became a constant vision
in my memory
I escape rough grounds to never live these broken moments again.

I remember lying on my back in a bed of mud
and the madness of the world crushed me -
I wanted it to die, but not I.

My eyes shut, terrified of seeing
the worst I'd pictured for myself,
afraid I'd get abandoned in the dark,
out of sight of triumph.
I haven't smiled in a hundred years,
my breathe slows down,
the air decreases,
my heartbeat drops,
time feels real, likes never before.

They found me half buried,
carried my hungry body
above the pretend graveyard
with caring embrace,
kind-filled-heart of bravery.
My breath revives,
my old life is lost in the past,
the madness has died at last,
I feel happy to be alive, it makes me smile
again.

Golden Bright

The past was once the best teacher
of my future.

In the present,
a distant and dark side of light
pulls suffering to the surface,
in a place where one smile feels
like millions of smiles,
and irradiates profound beauty
far beyond our sight
and brings peace to the world.

On a pale green wall of the hospital,
insipid yellow
pictures display long gone wars
and battlefields.

If your eyes see the same,
must I know what could make you feel better?
Must I sing through the tone of heaven?
Must I strum my heartstrings to make you rest,
dance and forget pain?

Injuries may seem weak on paper
yet all I see is a person's strength,
no memories or moments
may be long-forgotten in your history.

You are more than what I now see,
may the melody of my arms
rock your soul gently
may my music awaken the shine in you
beneath the darkness.

Silence

She sits at dawn and speaks
to the waves of the river,
she'd rather admire glowing water
than darkness in the woods.

The city moves around her,
a mind deep enough to find lost stones:
there is no place for a sinner
though heavy sentiments are yet to conquer.

It isn't that she lives
in a still life painting,
it's that she draws her thoughts before night-time
until they come out of sight
and suddenly, her strength
becomes the astonishing light of her shadow.

It's not that she intends to change the world,
it's that she shows me hers by simply living
a life without pretending
and that's inspiring.

The way she surrenders is beautiful,
shipwrecks, storms and battleships
without regrets,
leaving no time for a seafarer's nonsense.

Needless for words to express themselves,
to explain the seen and unseen world,
we capture long life observances
when she and I speak best in silence.

Hopeful Heart

It is not that I fell for you
When our eyes met
I felt the depth of your soul
Captured your essence
Understood my hopeful heart
Wished to find you again
And loved you in another life
As my love kept growing with time
Along with the distance that kept us apart.

Words of a Granddaughter

Grandma's Home

Grandma used to live a long drive away. The two hours it would take, I disliked very much although I loved looking at the scenery through the car's window. I'd listen to music and would dream endlessly. We'd visit her twice a month, and I adored sitting beside her on the rustic oak porch that wrapped around her home. It was a place forever serenaded with the gentle twinkling of wind chimes.

It was a modestly painted white house, in a quaint small British town, and a two minute walk from a crystal clear river, a river where a family of ducks had made their home, and we'd spend hours feeding them golden sweetcorn on rainy and sunny days.

She was wise beyond her years, and her voice was as comforting as the sound of piano music on a night pouring rain outside my windows. Perhaps she was the song I'd listen to, to conquer my worries.

She once told me she had had more than one lifetime to make mistakes and learn from them.

I'd often tell her about my dreams. I wanted to become one of the best ballet dancers in the world, go to an orphanage and teach children how to write, one day. When I was four, I told her, someday I'd visit the galaxy hoping I'd land on the moon, and I'd eat cheese up there. My dreams were often out of this world, and that was okay with me. She never judged me for it. It must have been something to do with the family kind of love. The one that's often lasting beyond the test of time, mistakes, and remain forgiven.

I wanted to reach for the sky to see what hides behind the clouds, to touch hearts and souls to bring them pieces of good. I dreamt of seeing the world and what lived outside of the small town my parents chose to settle in.

A few times, she told me I'd be an incredible poet; probably because quotes and music lyrics were my biggest life distractions, alongside daydreaming. She told me my books would all be different but would have similar themes. She said I'd have to start somewhere, learn as I go and would have to let go of perfection, we are only human after all. *She said as I learn, the second book would probably be better than the first one and so the rest would follow that pattern.* As a child, I was a lover of words. I'd spent hours every week reading quotes, music lyrics and word definitions. I seldom wondered what it was like to be a poet

though it seemed that they often understood life differently,
and so did I.

Grandpa always had chewing gum of different kinds. I could tell in his smile, when he'd offered one to me, that was one of his life's sweet pleasures. He was a good storyteller, loved playing acoustic guitar, and we'd sometimes talk about life's philosophies. He was full of survival and he knew I admired him for that.

Grandma taught me to listen and focus better by telling me her childhood stories and how she and her siblings would play hide and seek among fields of flowers until dark. She'd often tell me about her favourite painters, poets and musicians, Grandpa being one of them. She was musical, psychological and gentle. But most of all,
she was poetry.

Her tomato rice soup warmed my winters and I make it when I miss her a little too much along with the days of our history. It's the only recipe I've ever followed instructions to.

She loved drinking peppermint tea on cool summer evenings, and, now, I drink it all year round. Mum thought we were alike. Maybe it was the way we smiled, the way we cried or maybe it was simply that our souls were a little the same.

Grandma taught me a lot, even after she'd left. She'd talk to me about the boys I'd forget with time and to wait and tie the knot with the right one. Back then, I didn't know much about the heartbroken journeys that would lead me to him, and I was clueless of what that meant, what it felt like, until I met someone who I thought could be right for me.

Her perfumed red rose radiated elegant petals. It was true love from the moment she and Grandpa crossed paths. She mostly wore floral dresses on hot summer days. *Perhaps she was a timeless flower and will forever remain as the sense of earth within me.*

I don't know how long it's been since she faded but the remembrance of her essence, I would not describe differently.

Before she had to go, she said she'd told Grandpa I said hello. And perhaps, we'd meet in another life where I will, in turn, tell her about what I learned while she was away.

Or, perhaps, she left on vacation and will return in a decade or two, or I'll join her surfing when the sky turns green, and the grass turns blue.

She was right and knew it long before I did. During all these years, my heart has been filled with poetry.

Grandma's Remembrance

Pure white gold
with a tint of silver clouds,
ruby swan diamond,
she's a sincere piece of art.

Red rose fragrance
piercing the smell of her aura
painted clear sunset sea,
reflecting through her eyes,
melted tears, tucked in her skin,
enchanted smiles
sealed in her memory.

A defined beauty
with pure essence bones,
she's a mild sunny day
where firecrests come
to dream by the quay.

A necklace, suddenly heavy,
falling in wrinkled, soft hands,
after years of a well-meant life,
she's the evergreen in the elderly.

She engraved in my soul
the day her necklace became mine,
I then understood, she was the one
made of pure white gold,
now sleeping in stardust,
above silver clouds.

The Lessons I've learnt
The Family Tree

What I learnt from Grandma

Dreams

When no one hearkens
from a distance or near,
my feelings sing for my upset intellect.

My heartache finds the paths
where my dreams used to live,
and died freely and happily,
after they were softly killed by reality.

Where I dream of going,
I go, I walk
through the faith of my own window.

*To be brave and follow my truth

A New Path

I am sometimes reluctant
to explain the mistakes
I have made
and the reasons why
patterns never seem to break
after two lifetimes.

Suffering sometimes teaches me
to try again
to the best of my ability,
without trying to escape the Earth.

Though dilemmas in this way
do not fade,
I pause and ask myself
how may I stop
this replay in pathless hopes?

Decoding the mystery of infinity,
stopping the thoughts in my head
from spinning, I come back to myself
and begin again, detached
from the past,
as it cannot stay present.

Though I know I once taught myself
what not to do
and teach my insight
something new.

*To do my best to learn from my experiences

The Kingdom

When the shadow of sadness
embraces the sun in the village,
my eyes turn as grey as gloomy rain drops.

They sweep lost thoughts,
living as lonely as the invisible,
tucked in the world's most obscure secrets,
I do not tell anyone
about my night-time dreams,
they may frighten them.

My words left untold,
a sacred speech is yet to unfold
in imagery.

A penny in exchange for good advice,
a change of heart,
for a discovery in passion
leads me to read picture books of myself.

I once believed a place of happiness meant to sacrifice
wealth, though I was wrong.

If one could learn to love the imaginary and unborn,
I'd write an unknown plan and design a city
full of dreams in a kingdom of my own.

To embrace uncertainty and allow myself time to follow my passions and dreams. To find ways to make things work and live a creative life.

The Heart

Can one truly define regret
without making the wrong choice?
With time, often comes answers.

If one braves to be patient,
listen and discover,
can one live freely
from delayed decisions?

Can one dare to visit the unseen
in a world where superficiality reigns?
Explore deep and darkly horizons
before its scenery is revealed?

Though a choice may never be at fault
when choosing the heart's voice,
though regret may grow
where little devotion shows,
and fearful trust is yet to conquer.

*To live with as few regrets as I can.

The Meadow

Flowers shine in the meadow
reflecting the sun's troubles,
afraid of disappearing by the rain.

Roses grew two seasons late,
as such pace matters in a lifetime,
they held the soil of their ancestors,
they transform as they go.

I am a rose,
I need to cry,
I need to be watered,
I need to grow.

I break a piece of the earth,
it blackened my young soul's understanding,
then natural light enlightened my learning.

I once loved
the desolation of my past
observations,
my mind held to last
some of life's finest compositions
along with the ruinous strength
of self-destruction.

Troubles stem from being afraid
to stand alone,
loneliness hides a joyful mood
of independence,
I extricate thorns
and dress my roots
with red rose petals
and faithful confidence,
I stand tall and rise

among the rest.

In no circumstance,
should self-care be a test,
protecting myself from the wildest tornadoes,
I do my best
to not lose myself in thunder.

Once the storm is over,
I shine my brightest
in the disappearing rain.

* *To learn to take care of myself.*

The Oak Tree

There you stand, in a forest
of melancholic and majestic height,
your leaves welcoming the windstorm,
gracefully dancing
in relentless shadows.

The wounds of your pain,
reveal murmuring, forgotten conversations
you once had with yourself,
they are long lost.

Outspoken are the pages of your story,
the scars on your roots speak
of natural truths,
the mud surrounding you
disperses space for temporary refuge
to let you recharge,
begin afresh,
breathe comforting mountain air.

The echo of past sorrows
becomes tears drops
in a river where water lilies flow,
painfully.

Though the light often stems
from a rayless sun,
falling asleep at dusk,
it awakens daybreak with the softest
of pastel morning touch.

Still, in light or darkness,
you always inspire
an earthy place for souls to go -

when in search for inner growth,
to flourish in your solace,
rising above a mournful sky,
yielding strength from your shelter,
as the river parches.

* To be grateful for what I have, to enjoy the simplicity of life and to use nature as a constant doctor for peace of mind, and an inspiration to grow with confidence.

The Butterfly

My heart seldom dares to cry,
it beats between reasons and emotions
where my mind dances with intuition,
ignoring why footsteps are lost
in contradictory logic.

Little by little, the shades of my essence unfold,
sharing with the world
who I came here to be
while the beauty of an awakened darkness
sheds layers of my old skin,
where the colours of my integrity
commit to an ever-growing power.

The train of my thoughts
is travelling deep in my past,
and running ahead of my future's glow.

Beneath the mauve sky, I linger
on my chest,
on an oak tree I laid my fears to rest,
when in time,
detaching from a solid glue
to whisper into the wind,
a pale hue,
left to fly, and settle for a life
of liberty.

* *To let go of fears, open my wings and fly; set myself free.*

What I learnt from Grandpa

Words of Wisdom

By no means, be selfish
though hardships sometimes blind
the heart, the noise of others
distorting serenity,
offering us what one may forget,
the sound wept,
as silent as can be.

The world does not conceal
all the unfoldings of evils and heavens,
poor in attitude, rich in kindness,
life teaches me to choose with dignity.

I may need a reminder
at some point in the future,
when words and actions are to be reconsidered,
to return to this page of poetry
to retrace advice in my memory.

A man of wisdom once told me
to be as kind,
as I can be.

* *To be as kind as I can be.*

The Robots

I've lost a piece of me
in a mirror full of mirages,
illusions, reality,
sometimes roaming between
the present and my next lifetime.

My vision of the world is becoming blurry,
I must decide what I want mine to be:
my mind's beginning to speak on paper,
I am all at once a dreamer and a creator.

My cousin once taught me
to play a game in the woods:
seek, without seeking,
hide, without hiding,
we were silly kids,
telling jokes to strangers passing by,
making them laugh on good or bad days,
skipping and jumping to reach beyond
limits in the sky.

In the future, we sold our evening plans on eBay,
bought groceries and paid at virtual counters,
we were characters
on the internet and in real life,
we danced with robots by the sea at midnight
until their batteries died.

We'd leave them by the quay,
hoping the waves would swift them away
as far as they could, to never see them again,
so we could play in the deep
woods,
as children once, every often, should.

*To do my best not to lose my identity in
this modern world, to think for myself and
see through the media.
To implement technology in my life in
a wise way, one that doesn't diminish
humanity.

The Garden

The garden speaks truth
when it feels at home,
my ego is dying from bitterness,
the essence of hatred disguises the aura
of winter,
making time fall
into a sombre summer.

I move into a better atmosphere
between salty and sweet,
kind
and cruel,
I bury grief,
it rests on the Earth's pavement,
oceans, three flights away,
become nourishing water for all.

I am rivers of music,
playing from the heart
and singing caring lyrics
as I conquer battles of my own,
I gain victory through deeds
of subtle love.

Though countless times I've compared
the highs of blossoming tulips and lilies,
as one stems from the ground
and the other from trees.
I shall remember
daffodils gently fall too,
to blossom as new
and how flowers grow best
in a place of love and care.

** To live from a place of love and wanting
the best for others as well as* myself.

Covered by Mud

I found a lonely crimson leaf
suffocating
beneath shimmering sheets of mud,
in a forest as vacant as silence.

Doubtful of its worth,
I sunbath it in the river,
its bleeding scars
allowing light to shine through,
its broken pieces
reminiscing of the days
it was out of reach,
reigning on the throne of a tree
like the Queen of the Earth.

The water shed memories,
awakened hidden treasures,
and the map of its survival,
its breath existing in the dead noise
where its senses drowned to sleep
under heavy stones.

By its loneliness,
my heart held solicitude,
my sore eyes
reading the defeats of its history
in transparency,
admiring the blood-rose colour of a magnificent heart,
I am shocked it remains alive.

*To try to be compassionate.

Matter of the Heart

When I rest,
awake at night, I endure
the darkness
as much as I thirst
to disappear in it.

My heart, overshadowing joy,
my mind, abolishing sorrow.

The moonlight plays hide and seek
with the clouds as I sing
despair upon the horizon
and nourish myself
upon my voice's music.

Some may call me a fool to find peace
in melancholy
while others hear the same song,
capturing a rare beauty in solitude.

My pensive melody
draws blood in the darkly sky
and stops the overflowing,
deadly thoughts.

My pain is imprisoned,
wishing to be set free,
I embrace its tenacity
while my soul cries
for numbed senses.

The calm left in the world,
let me feel
an underlying tranquillity,

exhausted and zestful,
lonely and content,
solace in a mournful mood
of my heart's creation,
from an understanding sadness
and flourishing happiness,
making the darkness slowly fade away,
until I rise as the sun always does.

* *To be resilient, to learn to process my emotions and rise from the darkness.*

Autumn to Autumn

Through the month of October,
I admire the leaves' flurry
to meet a new home -
grounded
between the wind and autumn air.

The auburn sun waking me in mornings
from my deepest darkness,
in a quiet space of mind, I surrendered
and outshined the forest green
of leafless trees,
beneath their tragic black shadow.

A day in time, nature wears the costume
of faded orange confetti,
decomposing layers of ancient inner-self,
as a bright coloured painting turning into
a photograph from the nineteenth-century.

A soul growing in decadence,
breaking through the desert-dried soil,
iced among the wintered snow,
blooming towards pink-roses of spring,
learning to rise in its innocence,
transforming the scent of floral fragrance,
to arrive peached, ripped
at the end of summer,
guilty of outgrowth.

*To surrender, to keep learning and growing.

The Keys

The one who loses his keys
may not have lost his memory,
only nobody can lose nothing
because everybody loses something
every single day and night.

The one who dreams
loses nightmares
whether they mourn asleep
or think while awake.

The one who is frightened
loses calm
whether they conquer battles
or refuse to fight.

The one who feels happy
loses sadness,
the one who cries
turns dry cheeks to wet,
death loses life
and the alive lose time.

The who dares honesty
eliminates lies and confides.

Though, what is to remember
is one who loses
always gains
and one only truly loses,
when nothing is learned
from bitterness
and inside pain.

* *To overcome loss and embrace change.*

A New Kind of Dancing

The world is tearing me down,
my arms embrace oceans waves
and caress their enchanting music.

My feet flirt with the earth
and the emerald of eternity
overlooking the seaside valleys of the galaxy,
my eyes hypnotise lost victories.

The sky announcing foreseen chances,
the sleeping sun is on fire
and burns the soil of false wonder.

Its settling calm dispersing the mood of the night,
offering light to the darkness,
slowly becoming out of sight,
welcomes hopes of morning melodies
as the outshining stars look down on me
for tomorrow.

* *To move with the flow and always remain hopeful.*

The Melody

When my heart is in zenith pain,
my days of lively passion
become weak,
my smile is a delicate stream of tears,
meandering to waterfalls
which sing to charm my troubles
healing my innocent voice
of my immortal soul, inhaling the lavender field's scent
where I dance in harmony.

I am now free of hurt,
the comfort of music is a need
to surrender as best I can,
I flourish into the melody of early spring,
softening my torns under the warmth
of the low-lit sun.

The light awakens within me,
This story uplifts in joy,
in a garden where no flowers appeared before
but, now, lilies blossom
as lively as my heart's cheerful mood -
if only they'd known
how birdsongs could have helped them grow
if only they had listened,
they in turn would have learnt to sing.

* *Grandpa made me understand the power of music.*
How it can help me relax and release pain. He taught
me the depth of its value, that it is not only for enter-
tainment but for therapy. Music is one of the voices of
the soul, and we can heal through it, just like poetry,
art and nature.

A Granddaughter's Note

As I keep living with my imperfections and perfections, which make me the person I am today, the remembrance of my grandparents echos in my heart. They have taught me the value of life and the value of continuous growth.

My mother, father and I grew up in England and developed a shared loved for the arts, music, poetry and nature throughout the years. My mother must have learnt a lot from my grandparents, too.
 She taught me how to live as free as a bird with the thoughts of a wild-flower. She's done that by always giving the freedom to follow my own path in life and by never judging me for thinking for myself, and for doing my own things.

When my mum turned fifteen, Grandma wrote her a letter, which she then gave to me when she was ready to let go of it. Even so, I know she made a few copies of it then stored it in a treasure box I made when I was five years old and took a picture of it and emailed it to herself. *It makes me wonder if we can ever let go of the things that capture our soul and heart to the deepest of their core.* Perhaps the best 'things' in life are not tangible at all. *Perhaps, words, people or a place that feels like home are what truly moves us on the inside.*

With immense temptation, I read the letter for the first time the evening before my thirtieth birthday. I couldn't help to think that this precious letter should be read by anyone going through the ups and downs of life. It's a letter about never losing hope, believing in yourself, learning from your mistakes, letting go of fear and anything else that speaks to you when you read it.

It's a letter that shall be read in times of hopelessness or the need for comfort. Though, sometimes, I read it on random days or evenings before going to bed or when I awake in the night and I'm unable to sleep .

It's a letter that should be read whenever you need it.

Wildflower, I am

I welcome the ships and battlefields
of my existence,
letting them pass through me.

I dwell on memories contained
by deeply-rooted, unconscious thoughts,
my spirit urges for the sea,
I belong to the waves,
free and ever moving.

Sometimes gloomy under wintry clouds,
though always calm and joyful at heart,
I am an untamed voyage
sailing across curtains of rain
and golden-sun reflections.

I disappear in adventure beneath darkly nights,
always returning as an ever-growing wildflower.

Never Forgotten

A Letter from Grandma

Darling wildflower,

I hope this letter will endure the test of time along with your storms, struggles and celebrated moments.

I hope you never cease to find the strength within yourself to push through the darkness when you're in a place you're searching for yourself or questioning answers to everything in life, from the vision of the world to your own, to the reasons why paper planes never really fly and have zero passengers.

There was a time when I was searching for my soul and seeking validation from this outside world and all I really wanted was to be on my own and hide in an unknown part of the world that breathes on a solitary planet.

So, then I was alone, for a while, as if the earth had disappeared on me, and I was left wondering where the clouds and the sun had gone. I spent countless evenings in my room spilling ink (and invisible blood from the scars of my soul) through the typewriter and my quill.

Confusion lived in my veins but then I did my best to plant seeds of love and hope into the deepest part of myself.

Though, at times, I felt myself falling from the balcony of a heavenly sky and I thought to myself, I am delusional, to dream without limits and to believe in some of the things that many find impossible to dream about. Repeatedly, I felt misunderstood in this world with my idealistic approach about life.

Life will teach you the greatest lessons by making you face challenges and know that, sometimes, the roads will be long and, sometimes, they'll be fleeting in the blink of an eye. Do your best to embrace the journey and keep searching for what feels meaningful to you until you find it, then commit to it. Never stop dreaming, never stop achieving even the smallest of things, never stop trying.

Throughout the seasons, my heart and ego kept travelling back and forth, battling against each other.

I was worried about perfection -

which left me in a depressed state some nights as I was torn and swimming in indecisions, in an endless ocean. It lasted throughout the wintery days and followed me on rainy nights when I had to rely on myself and red cinnamon candles for wellbeing and independence. The flames were high and I was afraid of failure, rejection and disappointment in myself but I never ceased to seek the truth. I was left wishing under stardust, that their fire would burn my dilemmas. But they didn't. And then I thought if I asked for this, for a pain that attacks the gut in my stomach and one that feels as if it will never leave. But, my dearest darling, I've learned that nothing easy or difficult stays for ever. And I've held on, my love. And every time this pain came back to me, I'd grow wiser and stronger once it had passed.
It's as if I was a rose and needed to (cry) - be watered to grow.

Sometimes, I'd wonder where my life would take me, despite the failures and the unknown. When this life knocks you down, look deep within yourself, take a moment and pause, somewhere quiet, among the trees, where you can hear the birds sing or by wide windows that open up a splendid view of the city, reflecting on the world. Sit down, take a deep breath and join the birds, sing for them or get charmed by your silence amongst the busy city noise.

Feel the pain in the middle of your chest and feel your heart beat at the same time. Realise how strong you are.

Never close your heart to the ideas of endless opportunities, changes, small and unexpected miracles. Believe in the force of the universe and in your strength to overcome hurtful moments. Dance under the warmth of the sun. Pour your heart out on paper or write a letter to your future self. Do what you have to do to feel better. But don't let the downs of life stop or crush your dreams. Listen to the voice of your heart, think about what it said when you thought about the question and give yourself time to reflect on the answer.
Give yourself time.
Know that what is meant for you will never bypass you, live your life this way.

And, always remember, that to build your dreams, you've got to begin somewhere, sometimes. Dare to do so, despite the unknown outcome. Take actions towards your dreams and ambitions and let go of the outside that you can't control.

Don't you dare fail to believe in yourself. Process the pain when it hurts (dance, write, cry your heart out), sadness is not bad; it simply gives you the chance to feel joy, too. **Always aim for happiness, expansion and growth.** Choose a moment each year and look back at the previous one; **notice how much you've grown and know how happy that makes you feel.**

I urge you to find what puts your soul on a calm, peaceful fire.

What is it?

Go through the motions, be courageous enough to fail and try again. Learn to become resilient and find what makes you feel free and feel it through every bone of your body, and your mind. I warn you, this life can get intense, deep, crazy and it's full of madness beyond this universe, sometimes. But the most beautiful things in life flourish at their highest from the seeds of emotional and uncomfortable pain so as they do from exquisite joy. And when you allow yourself to see the simple beauty of life and find the feeling of peace within yourself, it's worth living for. Don't settle for less, embrace what makes you feel uncomfortable and brings you expansion.

Be proud of yourself because you make me proud, endlessly. Keep learning from your mistakes and never stop growing from the inside. And when the world throws you drama and misery or when you unintentionally drown in your doubts, remember all of the challenges you've overcome though you may find lots of them were through failure first.

We sometimes suffer through difficult times, yet shine at our brightest among the darkness and rise alongside the brilliance of the viewless stars. Picture yourself, when you were five years old, running up and down the hillside as you were a bird and I saw it in you; even if you'd fall, you'd get up again, over and over again.

You had your own kind of wings when you were a child, and I knew they'd only keep growing with time.
Picture yourself running up and down on the hillside, falling and getting up again every time and be kind to yourself.

Be brave, open your heart and *let it learn, eternally.*
Look at yourself in the mirror and hear me say, you are beautiful, courageous, kind-hearted and unique. Then say it to yourself, and don't let anyone destroy this thought.

A letter that's infinitely yours...

Acknowledgements

Dear Readers,

Thank you for taking the time to read my words, I am grateful.

A special thank you to my little sister (not by blood but by heart), Christina, who is my human diary and never questions any of my wildest dreams. Thank you to my older sister, Janick, for always believing in me and to my niece and nephews who inspire me more than they'll ever know. Thank you to my number one fan, my mother, for always making me feel like everything I write is beautiful and out of this world, even when I see the imperfections.

Thank you to my friends and family who never cease to believe in me, no matter my dreams, and for supporting me through my poetry journey. Thank you to my grandmother, "mémère Dubé" who inspired me to write this book, years after she passed away.

A big thank you to Amy (illustrations on pages 5,73,103 and Nina (illustrations on pages 9,45,75), who are incredible artists and took the time to create beautiful art for my book. Thank you to ganeero.art for designing my book cover, it's been a pleasure working with you.

With love & emotions,

Françoise Hélène

It is not the absence of melancholy
Though the overcoming process during
its complete presence
That allows me to fulfil my heart with
greater happiness.

Françoise Hélène

About the Poet

Françoise Hélène is French-Canadian and was born in New Brunswick, Canada. She lives in England where she finds inspiration through nature, music, art, life experiences, creative health research and spiritual growth. She began writing poetry in the winter of 2018.

An optimist who never ceases to learn from sadness and an out-of-this-world dreamer, she is a deep thinker and embraces both joy and melancholy but always aims for happiness and growth. She wishes to inspire and share her insight through poetry.

The Author

In October,
when the autumn leaves fell off the trees
and the world adapted to a new colour,
is the time my memory travelled to the place I grew up,
adventures that led me to the person I am today.
In the mild cold wind,
I breathe and swallow past moments,
one by one,
light and darkness; the laughs, the cries,
every movement.
I am so thankful for
who I am today.
The journey of a shy kid,
empathetic human mind,
my heart grew with it all,
a kind,
understanding,
heart.
I leave my past behind
without forgetting what it gave me
and I followed my destiny,
to where my future,
truth,
to find the comfort of home in a cup of tea.
That is how the rest of everything else began.